You Are Who
You Says You Are!
I Together
Don

Who Do You Think You Are?

How Discovering The Real You Unlocks Your Destiny

Don Roberts

To my wife and best friend, Nanette:
You're still the one.

Table of Contents

SOMEONE'S DESTINY IS DEPENDING ON YOU GETTING THIS

Your life is not your own. You belong to God, and He has great plans for you. He is determined to help you go beyond survival, realizing His full potential for your life. He has created you to be a person of great influence. And that is no small thing, believe me! Someone's destiny is riding on you getting this – because your life is intimately wrapped up in theirs. You may be very familiar with them, or they may be a perfect stranger to you. Make no mistake about it – your life lived out to the fullest will release them to be all that God made them to be. If you fail to discover who you are and what you are here on the earth to be, you will live a "less than" life, and that is not what God has planned for you. But it won't be just you that pays the price – people who you are destined to influence will also find their purposes short-circuited. So the stakes are high – but the rewards are worth it. By learning who you are, why God created you, and what He has for you to do while you are here on the earth, you will be releasing someone else to fulfill his or her destiny as well!

Proverbs 23:7 (NKJV)
"For as he thinks in his heart, so is he ..."

WHO DO YOU THINK YOU ARE?

CHAPTER 1

"Who do you think you are?" came the challenge from a little rooster of a man. He was a chain-smoking, dried up, bitter individual at the ripe old age of 25. Who knows what he had endured in his life, but it was obvious he had lost his ability to hope for anything better than this dead-end job. I had just joined the cleaning crew at the local shopping mall, working the night shift to earn a little extra money for college the next year. For me this was a beginning, a chance for a better life, and I was filled with expectations for my future. I would work hard, save my wages, and make something of my life. But for "Jim," my self-appointed boss, this was all he could see for his life. He was determined to do as little as possible, sleeping away as much of the shift as he could, and trying not to draw the attention of our supervisors. He had convinced the other workers of the wisdom of his ways as well, so I was not at all popular on this, my second night on the job. I had spent the previous evening trying to make a good impression, working hard and trying to do more than expected. Instead of earning the respect of my co-workers, I gained their scorn. I could tell something was wrong as soon as I arrived, drawing sullen stares and receiving only silence to my greetings. Apparently our overseers had noticed the fruit of my labors, and had been asking "Jim" why the crew had been able to accomplish so much more than usual. This had the effect of raising expectations, which was why "Jim" was challenging me now. What I found interesting, however, was the way he chose to pose his threat – challenging my identity – "Who do you think you are?" He was determined to put me in my place, to get me to play down to his level.

The temptation was real to learn my lesson and accept the counsel the guys had given me: remember who you are, and dial it back. I just couldn't do it though. It went against everything I'd been taught, and it felt dishonest to be sandbagging it. I worked hard the rest of the week, and was completely blindsided when I was called in to the boss's office and told they were letting me go. It turned out the veterans there had gone behind my back and concocted a story about my sleeping on the job, and how they had to do double duty to make up for my laziness! I couldn't believe it, but no amount of protesting on my part would convince the boss, and I was out of there.

You see, on the one hand, they had it right – it is critical to remember who you are, because who you think you are determines what you do in life But where they missed it was thinking my low position in the pecking order determined who I was. The fact is, whether I was the owner of the company, or the newest guy on the job, my identity was based on something far more important than seniority or vocation. I had to be true to my convictions if I was ever going to become who I was created to be. Dumbing it down, going along to get along, simply wasn't going to cut it. I might have fared better in the short term, but I would have paid a far bigger price later on if I had let others determine who I was going to be.

I know this, because several years later, as a young pastor, I completely lost my sense of self while attempting to keep everyone happy in my church. Inexperienced as a I was, through a series of events I had no way of foreseeing, I was suddenly elevated to the post of lead pastor at the tender age of 26. I had no idea what I was doing, and people knew it. Well intentioned, they offered advice to me regularly. They all seemed to have a different idea of what we needed to do in order to be a successful church. Usually their vision was based on some previous church they had attended, and they were relentless in their encouragement that if we just did what that last church did, we would be successful like they were. Naïvely, I attempted to do what they wanted me to do. If they felt we needed to start a ministry to a certain group of people, I did it. Program after program was launched, and we regularly tweaked our ministry style to try to do church like all the others did.

Before long, I was overseeing tasks I had no passion for, no expertise in, and certainly no sense that any of it was God's assignment for my life. The results were terrible. People were increasingly frustrated with my efforts, as I drifted further and farther from what God was asking me to do. I was depressed, people were leaving in droves, and I felt totally lost. Trying to be what everyone wanted me to be was exhausting, and all of my passion seemed to be drained out of me.

Eventually, I had to give up. It took me ten years of futility, but I finally went back to God and asked Him what He had made me to be and do. Only then could I begin to get a sense of purpose again. And slowly, lovingly, He began to show me what He had put in my heart. As I began to focus on the passions He had placed in my life, hope began to resurface. It was like being born again – again! I still had a lot to learn about leading God's people, but I had learned an important lesson. I couldn't be what others wanted me to be; I could only become the person God had created me to be. He knew me better than anyone, because He created me. Ironically, once His opinions became more important to me than what others thought, I became much more effective in helping others find out what God had planned for their lives.

What about you? Have you thought about who you are? Chances are, you've been challenged with the same question: "Who do you think you are?" What did you base your answer on? Other people's opinions? Your own accomplishments? Your dreams and desires? Depending on how you are wired, you may have a tendency to respond aggressively to that question, or shrink back. But stop and think about it for a moment – because your answer will affect the destiny of hundreds or even thousands of people. The truth is, you will interact with multitudes of people during your lifetime, and you will have an impact on many of them. Your actions will change them, one way or another. Consider your own life – haven't you been shaped by the attitudes and actions of others over the years? You probably remember comments made to you by a parent, a classmate, or a perfect stranger that wounded or encouraged you, and you've replayed those comments thousands of times in your head. Their assessment got lodged in your head somewhere, and you began to believe they were right, or you set out to prove them wrong. Either way, they impacted your sense of self, and had an effect on your life in a profound way. The problem is, people can't see you for who you really are, because they can only see what's on the outside. They see only a partial picture at best, but there is so much more to you waiting to be discovered!

So where do we look to find out who we really are? Do we look within ourselves; is that where the answer lies? Many have tried the route of self-discovery, but have ended up with a flawed view of themselves for their troubles. That's because we have no better idea ourselves of who we really are than others do, and for the same reason. Our perspective is limited, as if we are viewing life through the rear-view mirror. We can only look at what we've accomplished so far, and that often falls short of our hopes and dreams. Our past is a poor predictor of our future, but often we let it define us and limit us. That's tragic, not just for ourselves, but for all those whose lives God has destined us to touch. The world desperately needs us to see ourselves accurately, because the way we see ourselves affects the way we act, and the way we act impacts everyone around us in significant ways. A too-small view of ourselves will cause us to live in survival mode, instead of attempting the great things we are destined to do. We have been given the power to make a real difference in our world, but we live in ignorance of that fact. As a result, people around us are not blessed by our lives the way God intends. We need to settle the question of who we really are, for their sakes, but where do we turn for answers?

The truth is, God alone sees what is in your heart, who the real you is, and is the only one who can help you see yourself correctly. He made you, and He knows you inside and out. Look at what the Bible says about this:

> *1 Samuel 16:7b (NIV)*
> *The LORD does not look at the things man looks at. Man looks at the outward appearance, but the LORD looks at the heart.*

God's perspective is not limited like that of people – He sees what is inside you, and He knows what you can accomplish with His direction and leading. As your creator, He knows you better than you know yourself. The secret to understanding who you are is accepting God's opinion of you, rather than the opinion of others or even your own. When you agree with God about your identity, you will begin to make a positive difference in the lives of others around you. Make no mistake about it, God put you here for a reason, and He wants you to become a blessing to others. As He said to His servant Abraham long ago:

> *Genesis 12:2 (NIV)*
> *I will make you into a great nation and I will bless you; I will make your name great, and you will be a blessing.*

This is God's intention for all who give their lives to Him. Look at what the Bible says about this:

> *Galatians 3:14 (NIV)*
> *He redeemed us in order that the blessing given to Abraham might come to the Gentiles through Christ Jesus, so that by faith we might receive the promise of the Spirit.*

So what God said He'd do for Abraham, He will do for all of us who become part of His family through faith in Jesus Christ. If we believe Him, we will become the people He wants us to be, and others will benefit as a result. The problem is, many of God's people choose to believe their own view of themselves rather than God's. As a result, they live much smaller lives than He intended, and the world is a much poorer place for it.

Take Thomas Edison, for example. He is credited with more than 1,000 inventions, including the phonograph, moving pictures, the duplicating machine and, of course, the electric light bulb. Everyone benefits from his incredible inventions, but did you know he failed far more than he succeeded? Rather than let those failures define him, they merely motivated him to do better. He himself said, "I've not failed, I've just found 10,000 ways that don't work!" He went on to say, "Many of life's failures are people who did not realize how close they were to success when they gave up." Where would we be if Thomas had believed his critics who called him foolish and a failure in life? As a young boy, his teachers labeled him "addled" because his quick and inquisitive mind caused him to become bored easily with their rote method of teaching. In addition, he had serious hearing problems that further inhibited his performance in the classroom. What if he had believed those early pronouncements? By his own admission, if his mother had not begun homeschooling him and encouraging him to learn in different ways, he would have "turned out badly." But look at the tremendous influence his life has had on your own, along with millions of others! We **do** affect each other, sometimes in dramatic ways.

Abraham Lincoln is another example of this principle. Considered to be one of the most influential men to have ever lived, he experienced plenty of failures and had ardent critics throughout his life. In 1832, he lost his job and was defeated in his run for the state legislature of Illinois. The following year, his business failed. In 1835, his sweetheart died, and a year later he had a nervous breakdown. In 1838, he was defeated in his bid to become Illinois Speaker of the House. In 1843, he was defeated for nomination to congress, and after being elected to one term as a congressman, he was not re-nominated. In 1849, he was rejected as land officer, and in 1854 and again four years later, he was defeated in his run for the U.S. Senate. In between, he was defeated in his nomination for Vice President. Finally, in 1860, he was elected President of the United States. Even after his election, he endured a constant barrage of criticism on everything from his appearance to his job performance during one of the most critical times in the history of the United States. He did not let others define him, though, and all of us are benefactors of that decision.

Consider Rosa Parks, the extraordinary woman who made a simple decision that had a huge impact on our nation. You've heard her story. After finishing work for the day, she boarded a bus in Montgomery, Alabama, and headed for home. She was tired, and was no doubt looking forward to a quiet ride. The bus was crowded, and she was ordered to give up her seat simply because she was an African American. When she refused, her decision eventually led to the demise of institutionalized segregation in the South. Many consider that day, December 1, 1955, to be the beginning of the civil rights movement in the United States. Her act of courage inspired thousands to challenge the statement, "Who do you think you are?" Though we still have a long way to go in learning how to treat one another in this country, no one would argue that America is a better place because of the stand Ms. Parks took. She did not allow the ignorant or hateful to define who she was. Instead, she based her actions on a better understanding that God had created all of us as equals.

Your life story may be less well-known, and your influence perhaps less widespread. And yet, you **will** influence many lives by your actions. You will either be a blessing or a curse, but you will not be without significant impact. And your effect is completely dependent on your self-view.

DISCUSSION QUESTIONS

Can you think of one person's opinion that has shaped how you see yourself?

_____

_____

_____

How does that opinion agree or disagree with what God says about you?

_____

_____

_____

Is there a story you tell yourself in your mind that may not line up with God's view of you?

_____

_____

_____

In what ways do you think you are wrong about you?

_____

_____

_____

Do you believe that God is qualified to determine your identity? Why or why not?

_____

_____

_____

CHAPTER 2

GOING TO SCHOOL ON THOSE WHO'VE GONE BEFORE

CHAPTER 2

"Get your experience cheap," someone once said to me years ago. "You don't have to learn everything the hard way!" When I asked what he meant, he explained: "You can learn things a couple of ways. You can learn everything by personal experience, or you can learn through the experiences of others." The first way is effective, but expensive! For instance, someone tells you not to put your hand on a hot stove, lest you burn yourself. You can accept what they say, and avoid burning yourself. Or, you can go ahead and test their theory by touching it yourself. As you feel your flesh burning, you will have learned that – surprise, surprise– they were right! In both cases you learned, but the personal experience cost you more. Now admit it, haven't you learned this same lesson? How many times have you had a waiter tell you, "Careful, this plate is really hot!" and then went ahead and touched it anyway?

Me too, but after several fried fingers, I've learned most of the time to take their word for it!

Another friend told me, "I don't have any expectation of a mistake-free life, but I do want to be creative enough to make new mistakes!" The Bible backs up this way of thinking, and tells us that all of the stories recorded in its pages are to help us avoid the errors of those who've gone before us:

> *1 Corinthians 10:11 (NLT)*
> *All these events happened to them as examples*
> *for us. They were written down to warn us, who*
> *live at the time when this age is drawing to a*
> *close.*

With this in mind, I want us to look at the life of Saul, Israel's first king. I think we can go to school on his life, and hopefully avoid the mistakes he made. You see, Saul suffered from an inaccurate self-view, and it cost his people dearly. Thousands of lives were negatively impacted by Saul's stubborn refusal to see himself the way God saw him.

Even from a young age, Saul had plenty of "kingly" attributes. He was unusually handsome and looked like a leader:

> *1 Samuel 9:2 (NLT)*
> *...Saul was the most handsome man in Israel –*
> *head and shoulders taller than anyone else in*
> *the land.*

Saul knew that people were impressed with him. He suffered from the burden of potential, from other people's predictions of future greatness. Like many young athletes or child actors today, he felt the pressure of living up to other people's expectations. Instead of being encouraged by their opinions of him, Saul began to retreat from others. He based his worth on what others thought of him, and that mistake would haunt him throughout his adult life. He lived with the fear that he would be found out - that he wasn't the man people thought he was. Saul knew all too well his flaws, his limitations, his fears and frailties. Underneath that handsome exterior was a frightened little boy. But God had a very different view of Saul. He had a destiny for him that had little to do with his good looks or physical stature. He wanted to make Saul into a deliverer, one who would make the lives of his people safer and more fulfilling. God intended to make him Israel's first king, positioning him to free his people from terrible oppression. The Lord revealed His opinion of Saul to Samuel, who was leading the nation at the time:

> *1 Samuel 9:16,17 (NIV)*
> *[16]About this time tomorrow I will send you a man from the land of Benjamin. Anoint him leader over my people Israel;* ***he will deliver my people from the hand of the Philistines.*** *I have looked upon my people, for their cry has reached me. [17]When Samuel caught sight of Saul, the Lord said to him, "This is the man I spoke to you about; he will govern my people."* ***(emphasis mine)***

Notice how clear God was about who Saul really was – the deliverer of God's people. He was to be their leader. The people had been crying out to God for relief from the Philistines. They were a particularly cruel people who were conducting regular raids on the country, stealing and killing with abandon. Saul was to be God's answer to his people's prayer – but Saul struggled in that role, because he had a very different view of himself. Take a look at the following passage, where Samuel revealed to Saul what God had said about him:

> *1 Samuel 9:20b,21 (NLT)*
> *[20]"...I am here to tell you that you and your*

family are the focus of all Israel's hopes."
*[21] Saul replied, "**But I'm only** from Benjamin,*

the smallest tribe in Israel, and my family is the
least important of all the families of that tribe!
Why are you talking like this to me?"
(emphasis mine)

Did you catch that phrase, "I'm only?" How often have we said the same thing? We begin to dream of doing some great thing with our lives, but then we consider our shortcomings and begin to excuse ourselves from pursuing that dream by saying to ourselves, "Who am I to try such great things?" or, "I'm only (you fill in the blank here, almost anything will fit.)" We see our flaws, our lack of education, skills, experience, or resources, and conclude there is no use in trying. How many dreams die premature deaths because of this? It is tragic enough for us to miss out on the joy of achievement, but so many others end up losing out as well. Their lives are poorer for our holding back, and in some cases their dreams are short-circuited.

I experienced this pretty early on, while still in high school. At that time of my life, I had two passions: baseball, and (my then girlfriend, now wife) Nanette. As baseball season came around, I decided not to try out for the varsity squad, convincing myself that even if I made the team, I would be riding the bench. Our school was pretty loaded with great athletes, and I secretly believed I just wasn't good enough. So, I elected to stay on the junior varsity team, where I had been a starter the year before. I told myself it was all about playing time, but in reality, I was drowning in insecurity.

Now what I didn't know was the varsity coaches were looking forward to me joining the team, and had already penciled me in at third base. When I didn't try out, they assumed it was because I wanted to spend more time with my girlfriend rather than put in the extra practice time the varsity required. The junior varsity practiced one half hour later, and they saw me hanging around with Nanette during that time and drew their conclusions.

The coaches' frustrations were compounded later on, when the kid who started at my position was injured and was lost for the season. They felt that if I had just been there on the team, they would have had greater success. Their resentments carried over to the next year, when they absolutely refused to let me join the team, as I had in their minds let them down so completely the previous year. I was branded a slacker, and nothing I did could convince them otherwise. I wasn't good enough in their eyes, and unfortunately, their belief became contagious – for the first time in my life, I believed I wasn't good enough – and that would begin a battle that would last years for me.

This was compounded later on when, at college, my roommate decided at the last minute to try out for the baseball team. He was a good guy, full of confidence and seemed so carefree, but in my opinion was not nearly good enough to play college athletics. I was worried for him, frankly, but he wasn't in the least. He figured if he got cut, no big deal, but asked himself, "What if? What if I make the team? That'd be a hoot!"

Imagine my surprise when, a couple of weeks later my roommate came sauntering into our apartment, celebrating, having just been offered a position on the team. I couldn't believe it! Now my regret was compounded, since I realized if I had just gutted it out and risked it, I probably would have been able to play the sport I loved for a while longer!

It never occurred to me to try out, convinced as I was that I was not talented enough, even though, (in my humble opinion) I felt I had much more ability and experience than my roommate. I had let my regrets pile up, and had allowed my high school coaches' opinions of me to overrule my dreams of playing baseball.

Instead of learning my lesson from high school, I had just repeated it in college! But one good thing came out of that tough time: As I struggled to deal with my opinions of myself, I remembered how badly I regretted not at least trying, and this fueled my determination to change my mind about me! I vowed to never again fail for lack of trying! I've failed plenty of times since then, but rarely for shrinking back from the challenge ahead. I've found that the pain of regret is so much greater than failing while giving it my all.

I had made the same mistake Saul did, failing to learn from those who had gone before me. Had I known his story then, I might have avoided all that anxiety and pain.

It wasn't just Saul who paid the price for his identity problems – his people suffered as well. God wanted them to live free from oppression, and had selected Saul to deliver them. But he just couldn't believe God would use him in that way – in his mind he just wasn't the man for the job. He believed he knew better than God who he was. Saul held that view throughout his entire reign as king, at great cost to himself, his family, and his nation. God gave Saul all he would need to fulfill his destiny, but still Saul would not change his mind about his own identity.

DISCUSSION QUESTIONS

What mistakes did King Saul make in determining his identity?

_____

_____

_____

What did he base his judgments on; God's statement about him or the opinion of others?

_____

_____

_____

Think of an instance where you have done the same thing – allowing what others think about you to overrule what God has said. What happened?

_____

_____

_____

What "I'm Only" statements do you tell yourself?

_____

_____

_____

YOU'VE GOT WHAT IT TAKES

CHAPTER 3

From the beginning of Saul's assignment as Israel's deliverer, God equipped him with everything he would need to succeed. After declaring him to be God's choice as deliverer of His people, Samuel began to give Saul very specific instructions. Within those instructions we see all the necessary ingredients for success:

> *1 Samuel 10:4-9 (NIV)*
> *[4]They will greet you and offer you two loaves of bread, which you will accept from them. [5]"After that you will go to Gibeah of God, where there is a Philistine outpost. As you approach the own, you will meet a procession of prophets coming down from the high place with lyres, tambourines, flutes and harps being played before them, and they will be prophesying. [6]The Spirit of the LORD will come upon you in power, and you will*

prophesy with them; and you will be changed
into a different person. [7]Once these signs are
fulfilled, do whatever your hand finds to do, for
God is with you. [8]"Go down ahead of me to
Gilgal. I will surely come down to you to sacrifice
burnt offerings and fellowship offerings, but you
must wait seven days until I come to you and tell
you what you are to do." [9]As Saul turned to leave
Samuel, God changed Saul's heart, and all these
signs were fulfilled that day.

The first thing Saul was given was loaves of bread. How could that possibly be helpful? What does the bread represent? Jesus tells us that He Himself is the bread of life, and that He is all we need in order to accomplish what God asks us to do:

> *John 6:35 (NIV)*
> *Then Jesus declared, "I am the bread of life.*
> *He who comes to me will never go hungry, and*
> *he who believes in me will never be thirsty.*

If we eat of the bread of life, we will never go hungry, and we will lack nothing. Without Him in our lives, we will always be left feeling hungry. Even our accomplishments will seem flat and unfulfilling. We can dedicate our whole lives to achieving certain goals, and even accomplish many of them, only to find there's not enough reward to justify the effort it took to attain them. It's like the age-old saying, "I've been climbing the ladder of success, only to find it was leaning against the wrong building!"

How about you? Have you found yourself feeling rudderless, drifting from one experience to the next with no real purpose in life? That happens because our perspective is so limited, and we tend to choose the temporal over the eternal. We simply don't have the ability on our own to see what is really important in the big scheme of things. But God does see it all, and knows the very best use of our lives. His ways really are better than ours, and He is willing to share them with us if we will but ask:

> *Isaiah 55:8-9 (NLT)*
> *[8]"My thoughts are completely different from yours," says the LORD. "And my ways are far beyond anything you could imagine. [9]For just as the heavens are higher than the earth, so are my ways higher than your ways and my thoughts higher than your thoughts.*

Jesus stands ready and willing to share God's plan for your life with you. He is the key to understanding your purpose in life, and to comprehending your true identity:

> *Matthew 11:28-29 (NLT)*
> *[28]Then Jesus said, "Come to me, all of you who are weary and carry heavy burdens, and I will give you rest. [29]Take my yoke upon you. Let me teach you, because I am humble and gentle, and you will find rest for your souls.*

The term "yoke" here refers to His purpose for our lives. He knows we have been created to want our lives to amount to something, to leave a legacy, to impact eternity. If we live our lives His way, that is exactly what we will do. You see, Jesus was sent to equip us to do great things for God, and He said we would do even greater things than He did:

> *John 14:12 (NIV)*
> *"I tell you the truth, anyone who has faith in me will do what I have been doing. He will do even greater things than these, because I am going to the Father."*

As long as we have Jesus in our lives, we will be able to accomplish all that God puts in our hearts to do, no matter how limited we may be in ourselves. It is a fact that without Him, we can do nothing:

> *John 15:5 (NIV)*
> *"I am the vine; you are the branches. If a man remains in me and I in him, he will bear much fruit; apart from me you can do nothing."*

> *Philippians 4:13 (NIV)*
> *I can do everything through him who gives me strength.*

We feel inadequate apart from Jesus, and we, in fact, are – but the good news is that we will always have Him with us when we surrender our lives to Him. As a result, we can do everything God asks us to do:

> *Deuteronomy 31:8 (NIV)*
> *"The LORD himself goes before you and will be with you; he will never leave you nor forsake you. Do not be afraid; do not be discouraged."*

Going back to Saul's story, we see that he was given the most important ingredient for his success first. The rest of what he was given helps us understand the methods of God, and how He wants to accomplish His purpose in us.

DISCUSSION QUESTIONS

How does the Word of God help you understand your true nature?

_____

_____

_____

What are some of Jesus' assignments for your life?

_____

_____

_____

What are you doing currently that are not a part of His plan for your life?

_____

_____

_____

IT TAKES A TEAM

CHAPTER 4

It takes a team to succeed in life. Even the most talented person needs others to help him succeed. God designed life to work that way, and this principle is evident in Saul's equipping. Look again at Samuel's instructions to Saul:

> *1 Samuel 10:5 (NLT)*
> *"After that you will go to Gibeah of God, where there is a Philistine outpost. As you approach the town, you will meet a procession of prophets coming down from the high place with lyres, tambourines, flutes and harps being played before them, and they will be prophesying."*

By sending him to Gibeah, God is reminding Saul that his assignment is to be the deliverer of his people from the oppression of the Philistines. His first task is to go right for the teeth of the enemy, but he will not have to go alone.

God sends a group of prophets with him. God's work always involves teamwork; He doesn't call any of us to fly solo. We are designed by God to work together with others, and to benefit from each other's strengths. When God gives us an assignment, He isn't asking us to do it under our own power or strength. He will always give us people who are strong where we are weak, who excel in the areas where we struggle.

I've certainly seen this principle at work in my own life. I've been given the privilege of leading a wonderful church, and one of the things we are known for is our worship experience. While I love to worship, I have absolutely no musical ability whatsoever. If it were left to me and my talents alone, our reputation would be very different. But God has graced us with a wonderful community of gifted musicians who are also mature leaders. They lead us each week in worship, and I am happy to follow.Alongside of them, we have a great group of people who understand all things technical, another area of great deficiency in my life! Then there are the folks who minister so well to the children and youth in our church family, and those who work hard to prepare the facilities for our meetings, and those who go out of their way to make everyone feel welcomed and help people get connected. I could go on and on, but you get the idea. All of these people are gifted in different ways than I am, but together we are serving our community as God leads us.

God wants us to work together, and in fact intentionally limits us to some degree so we will need each other:

> *1 Corinthians 12:12,14-18 (NLT)*
> *[12] The human body has many parts, but the many parts make up only one body. So it is with the body of Christ. [14] Yes, the body has many different parts, not just one part. [15] If the foot says, "I am not a part of the body because I am not a hand," that does not make it any less a part of the body.*

¹⁶And if the ear says, "I am not part of the body because I am only an ear and not an eye," would that make it any less a part of the body? ¹⁷Suppose the whole body were an eye—then how would you hear? Or if your whole body were just one big ear, how could you smell anything? ¹⁸But God made our bodies with many parts, and he has put each part just where he wants it.

If we understand this principle, we will not be threatened by the good people God gives us, but rather will rejoice that He equips us so marvelously! None of us can be everything to everyone, nor does God want us to be. Instead, he forms teams of people, each with their own unique strengths and abilities, so that together they might be able to do all that the task requires. Eyes are wonderful creations, but they are ill-suited for walking over stony ground. They can help the feet avoid the obstacles, but are not able to do the walking themselves. By working together, the body benefits and functions properly.

Saul was given good people right from the beginning, in that group of prophets. That would continue throughout his life as king, and yet Saul was always intimidated by the good people God gave him. Instead of welcoming them as essential ingredients for his success, he pushed them away. Because God was calling Saul to deliver his people from the Philistines, it made sense that He gave him great warriors to help him defeat his enemy. And God indeed gave Saul his very best, two men who had it in their hearts to help him succeed in all that he did. Those two men were his son, Jonathan, and the man who would follow Saul as king, David. They were mighty warriors, courageous in battle and extremely loyal. Instead of being blessed by them, though, Saul threatened to kill them both!

Initially, Saul was glad to have David on his side, but that all changed when the people praised David's accomplishments, attributing greater results to David than to Saul:

> *1 Samuel 18:5-9 (NLT)*
> *⁵Whatever Saul asked David to do, David did it successfully. So Saul made him a commander in his army, an appointment that was applauded by the fighting men and officers alike. ⁶But something happened when the victorious Israelite army was returning home after David had killed Goliath. Women came out from all the towns along the way to celebrate and to cheer for King Saul, and they sang and danced for joy with tambourines and cymbals. ⁷This was their song: "Saul has killed his thousands, and David his ten thousands!" ⁸This made Saul very angry. "What's this?" he said. "They credit David with ten thousands and me with only thousands. Next they'll be making him their king!" ⁹So from that time on Saul kept a jealous eye on David.*

Saul's jealousy grew until it was out of control. Before long, he gave the order to his son Jonathan to kill David. When Jonathan refused, Saul attempted to kill his own son:

> *1 Samuel 20:31-33 (NLT)*
> *³¹ "As long as that son of Jesse is alive, you'll never be king. Now go and get him so I can kill him!" ³²"But what has he done?" Jonathan demanded. "Why should he be put to death?" ³³Then Saul hurled his spear at Jonathan, intending to kill him. So at last Jonathan realized that his father was really determined to kill David.*

Saul then wasted the rest of his years as king chasing down David, attempting to end the life of one of the greatest gifts God gave him. Instead of using his army to rid his nation of the Philistine threat, he directed them on a wild goose chase to eliminate his best asset!

Why did Saul react this way? He didn't understand who he was, and who God made him to be. He believed he was chosen because he was the best looking, the strongest, because he was literally head and shoulders above the rest. In his mind, he could only stay in his position if he remained the brightest and the best. But the truth is, God didn't choose him for those reasons, God chose him because He wanted to! Plain and simple, God chooses what the best use of our lives will be, not us. He gives us everything we need, including great people, in order to accomplish His purposes. We don't have to be better than the people we lead, just confident that we are leading because God has asked us to. Understanding that principle is the key to success in life, and will lead to great freedom for us all. Instead of being threatened by better people, we should thank God for giving us such great team members to help us accomplish His purpose for our lives. This attitude is possible only if we accept God's view of ourselves, rather than holding on to our own distorted self-view.

CHAPTER 4
DISCUSSION QUESTIONS

Who has God placed in your life to help you succeed?

_____

_____

_____

Is there anyone in your life you need to look at again?

_____

_____

_____

Are there those who are different enough from you that they might be God's gifts to you?

_____

_____

_____

Do you sometimes feel intimidated by talented people?

_____

_____

_____

What adjustments can you make in your attitude toward them to better reflect your gratitude to God for making them a part of your team?

_____

_____

_____

YOU'RE NOT WHO YOU USED TO BE

CHAPTER 5

Let's go back to Saul's equipping for a moment, and look at the next gift He was given:

> *1 Samuel 10:6-7 (NLT)*
> *⁶At that time the Spirit of the LORD will come upon you with power, and you will prophesy with them. You will be changed into a different person. ⁷After these signs take place, do whatever you think is best, for God will be with you.*

Saul was told that the Holy Spirit would come upon him, and would become the source of his power and success. No longer would he have to try to be better than everyone else, nor would he have to achieve more than anyone around him. The Spirit of God would be with him, and would empower him to accomplish whatever God called him to do. The Spirit would literally change him into another man, a completely different person than he was before. Indeed, he was changed into a brand new man, and yet he never believed it. This may be the most tragic part of Saul's story. Instead of learning how to live God's way, he continued to live as if nothing had happened – as if he were still the insecure young man who sincerely believed he "was only" an unimportant, insignificant person. This caused him to waste his life, but more than that, people around him suffered greatly as a result. The Israelites were not delivered from their enemies, Saul was deprived of the services of great people like David, his son Jonathan's life was cut short and God's purpose for his life went unrealized. These consequences are so far-reaching, I want to talk more about them in greater detail a little later on. For now, let's turn our focus back on ourselves.

Aren't we often guilty of making the same mistake? The Bible clearly states that each one who surrenders his life to Christ will become a new person, and yet we live like nothing really changed in our lives:

> *2 Corinthians 5:17 (NLT)*
> *What this means is that those who become*
> *Christians become new persons. They are not the*
> *same anymore, for the old life is gone. A new life*
> *has begun!*

We have an opportunity to start fresh when we become Christians, to see ourselves as God sees us, and to act in completely different ways than we would have before our transformation. The problem is, we often fall back on old habits instead of determining to learn God's new ways of responding to the challenges of life. It can be depressing to look at statistics of sexual sin, marital failure, addictions and the like. Often there is little difference between the struggles of Christians and non-Christians. Does this mean God's ways don't work any better than our own? On the contrary, when we begin to conduct ourselves according to God's directives, we will see very different results. The trouble occurs when we identify ourselves as believers but rely only on our own thinking to determine our courses of action. We mean well, but our perspective and experience in life is simply too limited to guide us in tough times.

Take our response to stressful situations, for instance. Now, I don't know about you, but I can be a world-class worrier. When facing difficulties, I have a tendency to want to look at every possible thing that can go wrong, considering worst-case scenarios until all of my hope is gone. I try to pass off this worrying as just good contingency planning, but the truth is, I'm really just responding to my stress in an understandable, though completely unproductive, manner. All of this, in spite of the fact that I **know** what God says about the pointlessness of worry, in fact I have taught on it many times:

> *Luke 12:25-26 (NLT)*
> *[25] Can all your worries add a single moment to your life? Of course not! [26] And if worry can't do little things like that, what's the use of worrying over bigger things?*

This verse reminds me that what comes naturally – worrying – really won't solve anything. But knowing what it says, and applying its wisdom to my life are two very different things. It is only when I determine to change my response to what God tells me to do that I see a change in my stress level:

> *Philippians 4:6 (NLT)*
> *Don't worry about anything; instead, pray about everything. Tell God what you need, and thank him for all he has done.*

God anticipated our natural response to stress, and gave us a better way to handle it. I have the option of talking to God about the things that concern me, instead of bearing all of the weight myself. I can thank Him for all of the times in the past He has helped me deal with tough situations, and this gives me confidence that He will help me today, as well. When I choose to respond His way, I get **very** different results! Instead of feeling sick in my stomach, I begin to experience a sense of peace and confidence. Rather than losing sleep over my worry, I begin to think more clearly and am much better equipped to handle things. But the key is choosing His ways over my own.

I'm sure I'm not alone in this struggle. No one sets out to ruin his life. Often we make decisions that seemed like a good idea at the time, only to have those same decisions backfire on us. This is not a new problem; people have been experiencing this for thousands of years. Look at what the book of Proverbs has to say about this:

> *Proverbs 14:12 (NIV)*
> *There is a way that seems right to a man, but in the end it leads to death.*

Our dilemma becomes compounded when we realize that **all** of our ways seem right to us:

> *Proverbs 21:2 (NIV)*
> *All a man's ways seem right to him, but the LORD weighs the heart.*

If we put these two verses together, we see that all of our ways seem right to us, and all of the ways that seem right to us end up in death! Think about this for a moment – who ever gets up in the morning and says to themselves, "Today I think I'll ruin my whole life and the lives of everyone I care about; I'm going to dedicate myself to this goal from now on..."? And yet we see people do this very thing when they first take a drug that starts a devastating addiction, or begin an extramarital affair that ruins their marriage and alienates them from their children. Those decisions must have seemed right at the time, or they wouldn't have made them, but they produce very different results than they had hoped.

Nowhere is this more evident than when we insist on holding on to our own view of ourselves. When we follow Saul's lead, and say in our hearts, "I'm only," rather than accepting God's view of us, we will end up with so much less than He intended for us to have. He has changed us into new people, and we must learn how to live in new ways. He promises to teach us if we are willing:

> *John 14:26 (NKJV)*
> *"But the Helper, the Holy Spirit, whom the*
> *Father will send in My name, He will teach you*
> *all things, and bring to your remembrance all*
> *things that I said to you."*

Saul was given the Holy Spirit to teach him how to live as a new man, and God gives each believer the same incredible gift. God's ways are better than our ways, and they can be learned! The Holy Spirit, as helper and teacher, will guide us through our growing pains. He may do this by speaking directly to our hearts, or by impressing on us to read a particular passage in the Bible. He may use the voices of others, speaking through them exactly the right words at exactly the right time. Haven't you had that experience before, when a friend says something out of the blue that was just what you needed to hear? Or perhaps you were listening to a sermon, and it seemed as if the pastor had been reading your diary? How did he know you were dealing with that very topic this past week? I've actually had people come up to me after a sermon and thank me for saying something I know I didn't say! Evidently the Holy Spirit wanted them to hear something other than what I was speaking on that day, and made sure they heard the right thing for them. Sometimes it is more subtle than that. You may just have a strong impression to call someone or to go somewhere, and it turns out later to be really important that you did. It may be that the Holy Spirit was guiding you, though your actions at first seemed rather ordinary. These kinds of situations are not mere coincidences, but the Holy Spirit is speaking to you through them to help you. He is determined to teach you how to throw off the old ways and adopt God's ways instead:

> *Ephesians 4:22-24 (NIV)*
> *[22]You were taught, with regard to your former way of life, to put off your old self, which is being corrupted by its deceitful desires; [23]**to be made new in the attitude of your minds**; [24]and to put on the new self, created to be like God in true righteousness and holiness. **(emphasis mine)***

Notice that phrase, "***to be made new in the attitude of your minds***." It is vital that this change takes place in our lives, because how we think about ourselves dictates how we act. How we act determines how we impact people around us. If we are still viewing ourselves as we did before we became new persons, we will act as if nothing has changed in our lives. God has come to make all things new, and when we understand that, we will change the way we interact with people as well. We won't try to cover up our weaknesses; we'll be freed from the need to impress others. Instead, we will rest in the fact that we are born again, and we serve at His pleasure. Rather than competing with people, we will begin to cooperate with them. As a result, God's purposes will be accomplished in us and in those around us, as well.

Unfortunately, Saul never experienced this change in attitude. Even though everything happened that Samuel had predicted, he remained unconvinced. When Saul returned from Gilgal, his uncle asked him what Samuel had said to him. Notice what he chose to share about that incredible experience:

1 Samuel 10:15-16 (NIV)
*[15] Saul's uncle said, "Tell me what Samuel said
to you." [16] Saul replied, "He assured us that the
donkeys had been found." But he did not tell
his uncle what Samuel had said about the kingship.*

He left out just one or two important details, didn't he? He
didn't share about being anointed king, because he didn't feel
he was up to the job. He didn't want the pressure of being the
man God had destined him to be. The ironic thing is he felt
greater pressure, acting against his new nature. Instead of
embracing his future, he hid from it.

CHAPTER 5
DISCUSSION QUESTIONS

How has the Holy Spirit changed the way you see yourself?

_____

_____

_____

In what areas are you most changed since you became a Christ follower?

_____

_____

_____

What worries are you carrying that need to be converted into prayers?

_____

_____

_____

What part of your life needs a fresh start?

_____

_____

_____

How can you cooperate with the Holy Spirit to see needed changes take place in your life?

_____

_____

_____

STOP HIDING BEHIND YOUR BAGGAGE

CHAPTER 6

The time soon came for Saul's coronation. In rather dramatic fashion, Samuel called all of the people together to prepare them for the arrival of their new king:

> *1 Samuel 10:19b-21 (NIV)*
> *[19] So now present yourselves before the LORD by your tribes and clans." [20] When Samuel brought all the tribes of Israel near, the tribe of Benjamin was chosen. [21] Then he brought forward the tribe of Benjamin, clan by clan, and Matri's clan was chosen. Finally Saul son of Kish was chosen. But when they looked for him, he was not to be found.*

Talk about ruining the moment! The suspense was building as tribes, clans, and families were eliminated from the race. Then, as Samuel finally revealed that Saul was the choice, he was not there! I don't know why, but whenever I read that passage, I picture Samuel as a presenter at the Academy Awards, saying "...and the kingdom goes to ... (drum roll please)....SAUL, SON OF KISH!" Great applause breaks out, searchlights go back and forth over the audience, looking for the winner, and ...and....and....he's not there! Backstage, the producers are scrambling furiously, trying to figure out what in the world is going on... you can almost hear the director of the show backstage frantically whispering, "Where IS he? I told you to make sure he was sitting in the front row so I could get the cameras on him! Go to commercial, quick, and find him NOW!!!"

Well, that's not quite how it happened, but you get the picture. They did ask God where Saul was, and he told them:

> *1 Samuel 10:22-23 (NLT)*
> *[22] So they asked the LORD, "Where is he?" And the LORD replied, "**He is hiding among the baggage.**" [23] So they found him and brought him out, and he stood head and shoulders above anyone else. (**emphasis mine**)*

What in the world was he doing there? The truth was, Saul was scared of being found out. He was overwhelmed by the pressure of potential, and, locked into his own perception that he was "only," he panicked and hid. He was sure he would fail in his role as king, and so rather than try, he ran. And look where he chose to hide – among the baggage!

Can you relate? We all have baggage in our lives, stuff we've been hauling around with us forever. Unresolved hurts, unfair treatment, confusion, bitterness; you name it, we've got it! And if we don't deal with our baggage, we'll find it is a convenient hiding place when we feel overwhelmed. We'll use it as an excuse for not trying. And when we don't try, we don't accomplish what God has placed us here on the earth to do.

That has far-reaching consequences for others around us, especially for those we care the most about.

Take a look at the following graphic:

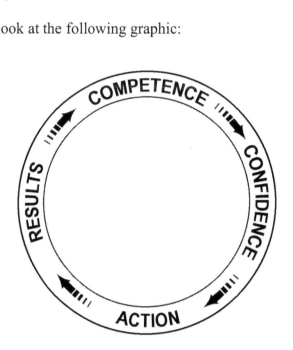

When we feel we are competent in a certain skill, we grow confident in our abilities. That confidence releases us to act on that skill, which then produces results that seem to verify our competency. The more we act, the more results we get, and the more we and others agree we are competent. Thus, both our self confidence and other people's confidence in us grow, spurring us to further action. God has designed us to live in this cycle of life. He makes us competent in Christ, not in ourselves. Once we understand this simple principle, we will live in this circle of competency. The problem occurs, however, when we begin to believe we are not competent in a particular area. That then launches us into a similar, but devastating cycle:

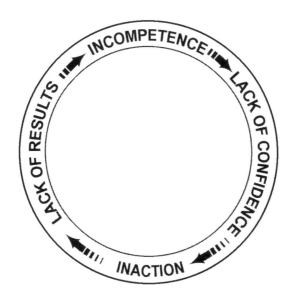

Let me illustrate what I mean by this. My mother suffered for years from emphysema, which severely reduced her competency in breathing. Most of us take our competency in this area for granted, and as a result, we confidently breathe in and out without giving the process a second thought. If we go running and find ourselves out of breath, we don't panic, we simply stop to rest, confident that our breathing will return to normal. For my mother, however, difficult breathing was a way of life. She **knew** she was not a competent breather, so if she got out of breath, it could become a serious problem. It was easy for her to lose confidence in her ability to breathe, and that could cause her to hyperventilate, which would make the problem worse. She could quickly end up living in the second cycle, afraid to breathe normally, and the result was less efficient breathing. On a few occasions, this would become so serious that we would end up in the hospital, getting medical treatment for her. Needless to say, this impacted all of us who loved her in a significant way. The solution was to get her to slow down, breathe as normally as possible, to return to the competency – confidence – action – result cycle. As she learned to trust this advice, she was better able to manage her fear of not breathing.

Think about your own life for a moment. In what areas are you the most confident? Where do you tend to hold back? If you examine those situations, you will find you are most confident where you feel the most competent.

As we return to Saul's life, we'll see how his inability to see himself correctly caused him to live in the wrong cycle. This had serious consequences for his people, especially for his own family.

CHAPTER 6
DISCUSSION QUESTIONS

What baggage are you still carrying?

_____

_____

_____

In what areas are you most competent?

_____

_____

_____

Where do you feel the least capable?

_____

_____

_____

Overall, would you say you are living in the Competency
Cycle or the Incompetency Cycle?

_____

_____

_____

OWNING YOUR IMPACT

CHAPTER 7

Remember what God said about Saul? He was to be the people's deliverer – setting them free from the oppression of their enemies:

> *1 Samuel 9:16 (NLT)*
> *"About this time tomorrow I will send you a man from the land of Benjamin. Anoint him to be the leader of my people, Israel. He will rescue them from the Philistines, for I have looked down on my people in mercy and have heard their cry."*

God's intention all along was to use Saul to alleviate the suffering of his people. If Saul had chosen to believe that God was right, the people would, indeed, be set free. But as we've seen, Saul held onto his own view of himself instead, and as a result, the people continued to suffer at the hands of the Philistines. Instead of being the deliverer, he ended up fulfilling his own vision for his life. He "was only" a victim, only an insecure man, only a defeated warrior, only a man whose life was cut short and whose destiny went unrealized. Saul eventually died on the field of battle at the hands of the very enemy he was called to defeat. That would be lesson enough for us, but so many others suffered due to this fateful decision. Because the Philistines were not subdued, they continued to harass his people for years to come. Israel's sons had to be drafted into the army, and many lost their lives in the constant skirmishes:

> *1 Samuel 14:52 (NLT)*
> *The Israelites fought constantly with the Philistines throughout Saul's lifetime. So whenever Saul saw a young man who was brave and strong, he drafted him into his army.*

This continued well into the next generation, and it wasn't until King Solomon's reign, some eighty years later, that they finally were delivered. How many lives were forever altered, unnecessarily, because Saul could not believe God's call on his life? His own son, Jonathan, died at his side, defending his father to the end. That event cost God's people further, in ways that might not seem obvious at first glance. Jonathan's premature death robbed Saul's successor, King David, of a great friend, trusted advisor and chief of staff.

Jonathan and David became good friends early on. They had much in common – both were fierce warriors, full of courage and willing to take risks to save the people they led. It may be those shared traits that became the basis for their deep friendship. At the time of their first meeting, though they were young, they had already achieved a measure of fame for their courage. Jonathan took on an entire garrison of the Philistines with just his armor bearer to back him up. David had just finished taking down the giant Goliath with his slingshot. They both had a deep trust in the Lord, and saw His abiding presence as the key to their victories. Notice the similarities in their statements while facing their enemies:

> *1 Samuel 14:6 (NKJV)*
> *Then Jonathan said to the young man who bore his armor, "Come, let us go over to the garrison of these uncircumcised; it may be that the LORD will work for us. For nothing restrains the LORD from saving by many or by few."*

Jonathan understood that victories came when warriors put their trust in the Lord. So did David – look at his statement while facing down Goliath:

> *1 Samuel 17:45-47 (NIV)*
> *[45]David said to the Philistine, "You come against me with sword and spear and javelin, but I come against you in the name of the LORD Almighty, the God of the armies of Israel, whom you have defied. [46]This day the LORD will hand you over to me, and I'll strike you down and cut off your head. Today I will give the carcasses of the Philistine army to the birds of the air and the beasts of the earth, and the whole world will know that there is a God in Israel. [47]All those gathered here will know that it is not by sword or spear that the LORD saves; for the battle is the LORD'S, and he will give all of you into our hands."*

Their actions took incredible courage, and in fact would have been foolhardy if they had not believed that the Lord would fight for them. In fact, these actions inspired the armies of Israel and gave them the will to fight the Philistines. With such similar leadership qualities, it is no surprise that Jonathan and David became instant friends:

1 Samuel 18:1,3,4 (NLT)
[1]After David had finished talking with Saul,
he met Jonathan, the king's son. There was an
immediate bond of love between them, and they
became the best of friends. [3]And Jonathan made
a special vow to be David's friend, [4]and he sealed
the pact by giving him his robe, tunic, sword, bow,
and belt.

Could it be that Jonathan recognized God's call on David's life? By giving David his royal robe, is he recognizing that David is to be the next king after his father, Saul? If so, as David's most trusted friend, he would have most likely been selected to be chief of staff of the new administration. This could have made a major difference for David, since his eventual choice for that role, a man named Joab, disobeyed him and even killed allies and David's own son against his wishes.

After Saul's death, David was God's choice to be the next king of Israel. But it was necessary for David to reach out to those who were still loyal to Saul. These people would have naturally assumed one of Saul's family would become his successor, since that was the custom of the day. They would need to be convinced it was in their best interests to agree with God's choice rather than the candidates they were backing. During this transitional time, a powerful man named Abner came to David and offered to support him. Abner became an influential force among those who were committed to Saul's dynasty, and David welcomed his offer for help:

2 Samuel 3:12-13 (NLT)
[12]Then Abner sent messengers to David, saying,
"Let's make an agreement, and I will help turn the
entire nation of Israel over to you." [13]"All right,"
David replied ...

2 Samuel 3:21 (NLT)
Then Abner said to David, "Let me go and call
all the people of Israel to your side. They will
make a covenant with you to make you their
king. Then you will be able to rule over everything
your heart desires." So David sent Abner safely
on his way.

Joab, however, disagreed with David's decision, and, instead
of supporting his king, went behind his back and murdered
Abner:

2 Samuel 3:26, 27 (NLT)
[26] Joab then left David and sent messengers to
catch up with Abner. They found him at the pool
of Sirah and brought him back with them. But
David knew nothing about it. [27] When Abner
arrived at Hebron, Joab took him aside at the
gateway as if to speak with him privately. But
then he drew his dagger and killed Abner in
revenge for killing his brother Asahel.

Joab acted in his own best interests, with no regard to how this
would affect David or his new kingdom. This hideous act
caused great political turmoil for David, forcing him to admit
publicly that he couldn't control his chief of staff:

2 Samuel 3:38-39 (NLT)
[38] Then King David said to the people, "Do you
not realize that a great leader and a great man
has fallen today in Israel? [39] And even though I
am the anointed king, these two sons of Zeruiah—
Joab and Abishai—are too strong for me to
control. So may the LORD repay these wicked men
for their wicked deeds."

Unfortunately, this rebellious trait continued, touching David's life even more personally when Joab murdered David's own son, Absalom. Absalom had led a rebellion of his own against David, and deserved to be punished, but David had expressed his desire that his son be reconciled to him. Instead, Joab again went behind David's back and killed Absalom:

> *2 Samuel 18:10-14 (NLT)*
> *[10] One of David's men saw what had happened and told Joab, "I saw Absalom dangling in a tree." [11] "What?" Joab demanded. "You saw him there and didn't kill him? I would have rewarded you with ten pieces of silver and a hero's belt!" [12] "I wouldn't do it for a thousand pieces of silver," the man replied. "We all heard the king say to you and Abishai and Ittai, 'For my sake, please don't harm young Absalom.' [13] And if I had betrayed the king by killing his son—and the king would certainly find out who did it—you yourself would be the first to abandon me." [14] "Enough of this nonsense," Joab said. Then he took three daggers and plunged them into Absalom's heart as he dangled from the oak still alive.*

The point is, if Jonathan had been alive, he most certainly would have carried out his friend and king's wishes, rather than go against him time and time again. If Jonathan had lived, he would have been a great support and trusted advisor, and Abner and Absalom would not have died prematurely. Those who loved them would have been spared their loss, and the nation would have benefited from their gifts and talents. Their leadership ability would have impacted countless more. All of these people paid a price, which can be traced back to Saul's refusal to believe God's destiny for his life. As we have seen, if Saul had simply chosen God's view over his own, the people would have been delivered; Jonathan would have lived, and would have lived out his destiny as David's right-hand man.

We can speculate just how far-ranging his influence as king might have been when we look at David's sin with Bathsheba.

> *2 Samuel 11:1-4*
> *[1]The following spring, the time of year when kings go to war, David sent Joab and the Israelite army to destroy the Ammonites. In the process they laid siege to the city of Rabbah. But David stayed behind in Jerusalem. [2]Late one afternoon David got out of bed after taking a nap and went for a stroll on the roof of the palace. As he looked out over the city, he noticed a woman of unusual beauty taking a bath. [3]He sent someone to find out who she was, and he was told, "She is Bathsheba, the daughter of Eliam and the wife of Uriah the Hittite." [4]Then David sent for her; and when she came to the palace, he slept with her.*

Instead of going to war with the army as he always had before, David lagged behind and made the biggest mistake of his entire reign. Had Jonathan been around, it is possible he would have gone to David and told him: "You can't remain behind, my king. You must lead your soldiers into battle. We must deliver God's people from their enemies. Now come, let us be going!" We'll never know, but this would not have been out of character for Jonathan. He shared David's love for God, his courage and his willingness to fight for God's people. David certainly would have been open to this most trusted ally. If you know the rest of David's story, you know that he not only committed adultery with Bathsheba, but had her husband murdered to cover up the fact that she was pregnant by David. His sin was then exposed publicly by the prophet Nathan, to his shame and humiliation. Even though David responded properly by repenting, he lost face with his people, and especially with his own sons. David's son Absalom later led a rebellion against his father, and it may well be this act that caused him to do it.

So we see that our decisions can have far-reaching, profound consequences and literally touch thousands of lives. How differently things might have turned out, how much suffering could have been avoided, if only Saul had believed God.

How about you? Are you struggling to agree with God about your life and destiny? Whose lives are being affected by your self-view? Are you willing to explore God's view of you, or will you continue to hold on to your own perceptions? Your answer is important, because you will affect many people, positively or negatively. You are designed by God to influence others, and He wants you to become a great blessing to many. You may not be a king or a powerful person in your own eyes, but God has put you on this earth to make a difference in the lives of the people you know and interact with. God has much to say about you, as we will see in the next chapter. If we can accept God's view of our lives, not only will we live much fuller lives ourselves, but our impact on those we come in contact with will be life-changing.

CHAPTER 7
DISCUSSION QUESTIONS

Whose lives are you most directly impacting?

_____

_____

_____

How does your self-view negatively impact them?

_____

_____

_____

What adjustments do you need to make to ensure a more positive influence on them?

_____

_____

_____

What statements has God made about you that you struggle with the most?

_____

_____

_____

Are you willing to explore more about who He says you are?

_____

_____

_____

YOU NAME HIM, HE NAMES YOU

CHAPTER 8

Jesus, like any good leader, asks a lot of questions. But unlike us, He is not looking for information when He poses His queries. Because He is all- knowing, He doesn't need us to fill Him in. When He asks us a question, it is to help us consider more deeply what we think. And nowhere is that more important than in the question of our identities. If we don't know who we are, we will struggle mightily to become all that He has designed us to be. If that is His endgame, you would think He would ask us the question we've been considering together: "Who do you think you are?" But He doesn't ask this; instead, He asks us a more important one: "Who do you say I am?" Your answer will unlock the truth about who we really are. Look in the book of Matthew:

> *Matthew 16:15-19 (MSG)*
> *[15]He pressed them, "And how about you? Who do you say I am?" [16] Simon Peter said, "You're the*

Christ, the Messiah, the Son of the living God."
[17]Jesus came back, "God bless you, Simon, son of
Jonah! You didn't get that answer out of books or
from teachers. My Father in heaven, God
himself, let you in on this secret of who I really
am. [18]And now I'm going to tell you who you are,
really are. You are Peter, a rock. This is the rock
on which I will put together my church, a church
so expansive with energy that not even the gates
of hell will be able to keep it out. [19]"And that's
not all. You will have complete and free access to
God's kingdom, keys to open
any and every door: no more barriers between
heaven and earth, earth and heaven. A yes on
earth is yes in heaven. A no on earth is no in
heaven."

Peter named Jesus as Savior and Son of God, and Jesus
responded by naming him a rock, solid and unmovable.
Peter's behavior up to this point would be more accurately
described as less steadfast and more impulsive, but Jesus
proclaimed who Peter would become as he followed Jesus as
Lord.

Jesus knows that your identity is tied up in His. If you don't
know who HE is, you can't know who YOU are. Why is that?
Because He made you, and you belong to Him:

> *Psalm 24:1 (NLT)*
> *The earth is the LORD's, and everything in it.*
> *The world and all its people belong to him.*

He alone knows who you are now, and who you are destined
to be. He knows what you and I must know: that we will find
our true identity when we agree with Him about who He is to
us. The apostle Paul said it this way:

Acts 17:28 (NIV)
'For in him we live and move and have our being.'

Look at how God is described in the Bible. This is by no means an exhaustive list, but it will give you an idea of who He really is.

He is our:

- Advocate, our lawyer *(1 Samuel 24:15 NLT; 1 John 2:1 NLT)*
- Almighty *(Genesis 17:1 NIV)*
- Author & Finisher of our Faith *(Hebrews 12:2 NKJV)*
- Alpha & Omega, the Beginning and the *End (Revelation 1:8 NLT)*
- Beloved *(Song of Solomon 7:10 GW)*
- Bridegroom *(Isaiah 62:5 NIV)*
- Bright & Morning Star *(Revelation 22:16 NLT)*
- Captain of the Lord's Army *(Joshua 5:15 NLT)*
- Chief Cornerstone *(Matthew 21:42 (NKJV)*
- Christ, our Messiah *(Matthew 16:16 NLT)*
- Counselor *(Isaiah 9:6 NIV)*
- Creator *(Isaiah 40:28 MSG)*
- Deliverer *(2 Samuel 22:2 NIV)*
- Emmanuel, God w/Us *(Matthew 1:23 MSG)*
- Eternal Life Giver *(John 17:2 NLT)*
- Everlasting Father *(Isaiah 9:2 NLT)*
- Faithful & True *(Revelation 3:14 NIV)*
- Firstborn of the Dead *(Colossians 1:18 NIV)*
- Friend of Sinners *(Luke 7:34 NLT)*
- Friend that sticks closer than a brother *(Proverbs 18:24 NKJV)*
- Gift of God *(John 4:10 NIV)*
- Good Shepherd *(John 10:11 NLT)*
- God above all gods *(Psalm 135:5 NLT)*
- Head of the Church *(Ephesians 1:22 NIV)*
- High Priest *(Hebrews 5:10 NLT)*

- Hiding Place *(Psalm 32:7 NIV)*
- Holy One *(1 Samuel 2:2 NIV)*
- Horn of Salvation *(2 Samuel 22:3 NIV)*
- The Great "I AM" *(Exodus 3:14 NIV)*
- Jehovah *(Psalm 83:18 KJV)*
- Jesus our Lord *(Acts 20:21 NIV)*
- Judge *(1 Chronicles 16:33 NIV)*
- King of Glory *(Psalm 24:8 NLT)*
- King of Saints *(Revelation 15:3 NKJV)*
- King of all the Earth *(Psalm 47:7 NKJV)*
- King of Kings *(1 Timothy 6:15 NIV)*
- Lamb of God *(John 1:29 GW)*
- Life *(John 14:6 NLT)*
- Life Giver *(Psalm 36:9 NCV)*
- Light of the World *(John 8:12 NIV)*
- Lion of the Tribe of Judah *(Revelation 5:5 NLT)*
- Living Stone *(1 Peter 2:4 NIV)*
- Lord of Lords *(Deuteronomy 10:17 NIV)*
- Man of Sorrows *(Isaiah 53:3 NIV)*
- Master *(2 Samuel 7:22 MSG)*
- Mediator *(1 Timothy 2:5 NIV)*
- Mighty One *(Genesis 49:24 NIV)*
- Only Wise God *(Romans 16:27 NLT)*
- Power *(Jeremiah 10:6 NLT)*
- Physician *(Luke 5:31 NLT)*
- Precious One *(1 Peter 2:6 NIV)*
- Prince of Peace *(Isaiah 9:6 NIV)*
- Peace that Passes Understanding *(Philippians 4:7 NKJV)*
- Prophet *(Acts 3:22,23 NLT)*
- Propitiation *(Romans 3:25 NKJV)*
- Protector *(1 Peter 2:25 NCV)*
- Provider *(Psalm 54:4 GW)*
- Rabbi *(John 1:49 NLT)*
- Ransom *(1 Peter 1:20 NLT)*
- Redeemer *(Psalm 19:14 NIV)*
- Resurrection & Life *(John 11:25 NIV)*

- Redemption *(1 Corinthians 1:30 NIV)*
- Righteousness *(1 Corinthians 1:30 GW)*
- Rock *(1 Samuel 2:2 NIV)*
- Ruler *(2 Chronicles 13:12 NCV)*
- Salvation *(Acts 4:12 NIV)*
- Sanctifier *(Ezekiel 20:12 NKJV)*
- Sanctuary *(Psalm 9:9 MSG)*
- Savior *(Exodus 15:2 GW)*
- Servant *(Matthew 20:28 NLT)*
- Son of God *(Mark 1:1 NIV)*
- Sure Foundation *(Isaiah 28:16 NIV)*
- Teacher *(Mark 14:14 NIV; Matthew 11:29 NLT)*
- Truth, Way and Life *(John 14:6 NIV)*
- Unspeakable Gift *(2 Corinthians 9:15 KJV)*
- Unchangeable God *(James 1:17 NLT)*
- Vine *(John 15:1 NIV)*
- Which is, Which was, Which is to come *(Revelation 1:4 NKJV)*
- Wisdom *(1 Corinthians 1:24 NLT)*
- Witness *(John 8:18 NLT)*
- Wonderful *(Isaiah 9:6 NIV)*
- Word of Life *(Philippians 2:16 NLT)*

That's who He is! And if He is all that, He is qualified to define your identity. He who created you knows you best, inside and out.

When you agree with Him about who He is, you position yourself to let Him name you for who He has made you to be. In effect, when you name Him, He names you. By recognizing Him to be the Christ, the Messiah, the Son of the living God, you are agreeing that you belong to Him. You are no longer living as an independent being, determining who you are and what you do. When you submit to His ownership, you acknowledge His right to name you. And rather than put you into bondage as His slave, He sets you free to be who He intended you to be all along.

His proclamation of who you are will set you free, freer than you've ever been, to be the real you; no secrets, no lies, no exaggerations. Simply put, you can declare: "This is me, the real me. And I am loved. Completely. Without reservation. On my best day. On my worst day. I am loved." And so you are, my friend, so you are.

You are a new creature, no longer bound by the things that have wounded you. Not because your behavior has improved, but rather because He has delivered you from all of that. The lie is broken for you, having been stripped of its power by the truth. You are made whole in Jesus. Even with all of your stuff, you matter. You matter to God. With each new day, you are becoming a better reflection of who you really are. You are on your way, loved one. Believe it!

DISCUSSION QUESTIONS

Who is Jesus in your life?

_____

_____

_____

What is the one most accurate thing you can say about who He is to you?

_____

_____

_____

Who do you think Jesus thinks you are?

_____

_____

_____

What is the single adjective He would use to describe you?

_____

_____

_____

GOD'S OPINION OF YOU IS THE ONLY ONE THAT MATTERS

CHAPTER 9

David was a man who held a far different view of himself than did Saul. He understood that only God knew the real David, and rejoiced that God would shape him into the man He wanted him to be. He discovered that his worth was not found in his own abilities, but rather in the fact that God had made him. Look at his words in Psalm 139:

> *Psalm 139:1-6 (NLT)*
> *[1]LORD, you have examined my heart and know everything about me. [2]You know when I sit down or stand up. You know my every thought when far away. [3]You chart the path ahead of me and tell me where to stop and rest. Every moment you know where I am. [4]You know what I am going to say even before I say it, LORD. [5]You both precede and follow me. You place your hand of blessing*

on my head. ⁶Such knowledge is too wonderful
for me, too great for me to know!

David acknowledged that he could not grasp all there was to
know about himself, but trusted His God who does know all!
As a result of that trust, his opinion of himself matched God's:

> *Psalm 139:13-14 (NIV)*
> *¹³For you created my inmost being; you knit me*
> *together in my mother's womb. ¹⁴I praise you*
> *because I am fearfully and wonderfully made;*
> *your works are wonderful, I know that full well.*

Notice the praise was directed to God, not himself, as he
marveled at God's great handiwork. The fact that he was
speaking of himself was not the point; he recognized he was
the created one, and only God could craft something so
complex and wonderful as a human being. David was simply
agreeing with God's opinion about his creation: man. God,
too, at the beginning of the world, stepped back after creating
man and enjoyed what he had made:

> *Genesis 1:31 (NLT)*
> *Then God looked over all he had made, and he*
> *saw that it was excellent in every way.*

As a result of that agreement, David was able to confidently
lead his people to victory after victory. He consistently
displayed courage and appreciation for the people God had
given him. David was as flawed a man as Saul, perhaps even
more so, and yet God called David a "man after his own
heart." Why was that? Because David chose to agree with
God's opinion of himself, rather than accepting his own view.
He understood the source of his worth was in the context of
his relationship with his Maker. He understood, as Proverbs
21:31 says, that "victory belongs to the Lord," and that God
was qualified to decide who served in what capacity. He

simply lived to do the Father's will. And that pleased the Lord immensely!

Think about what determines the value of artwork in our world today. Is the price of a painting determined by the cost of the raw materials used? Or is it computed by the number of hours the artist spent creating it? By these standards, even masterpieces would be affordable to the masses. But the truth is, some of these paintings are priceless. What makes the difference? Well, in some cases, it is due to the extraordinary talent of the artist, but beauty is in the eye of the beholder. What may be beautiful to me may not attract your eye at all. I myself do not happen to be a fan of Picasso's work. I simply do not see the genius some see in his creations. But let me assure you, if you were to give me an original painting of his, I would take great care with it. I would insure it, protect it, perhaps even lock it away in a vault where it's value would be preserved. Why? Because *I* think it is beautiful? Certainly not! But even though I have no appreciation for his talent, I would protect it and preserve it because it has great value on the open market. The value of the piece, then, is determined by what others are willing to pay for it. Though I would not pay good money for it, others would pay exorbitant sums to possess it. For this reason, it is valuable to me.

Why is this important? Well, you may not think much of yourself and your abilities. Left to your own evaluation, you might set a fairly low price on your worth. But in God's eyes, you are His masterpiece! He paid an outrageous price for you, spending the most expensive commodity in the universe on you – the blood of Christ! The rarest of all elements, His own Son's blood was the fee He paid for you:

> *1 Peter 1:18-19 (NLT)*
> *18For you know that God paid a ransom to save you from the empty life you inherited from your ancestors. And the ransom he paid was not mere*

gold or silver. [19]He paid for you with the precious lifeblood of Christ, the sinless, spotless Lamb of God.

We know that the more rare a thing is, the more valuable it is. If there is only one item in the world, it becomes priceless. So it is with Jesus' blood. As the only sinless being in the universe, His blood is more rare than any other substance in existence. And since God paid that high a price for you, your value is now priceless, as well. It doesn't matter whether you like yourself or not, or whether you think He overpaid, your value is determined by the price paid for you. Like a Picasso painting, you may not like what you see, but you are incredibly valuable nonetheless!

God wants you to understand that He alone knows your true value, and He alone is authorized to assign your life's work to you. Look at what the apostle Paul wrote in his letter to the Ephesians:

> *Ephesians 2:10 (NLT)*
> *For we are God's masterpiece. He has created us anew in Christ Jesus, so that we can do the good things he planned for us long ago.*

God has great things for you to accomplish, and wants to influence many lives through you. It is vital, therefore, that you learn to agree with Him about who you are and what your purpose in life is. As we have seen from the life of Saul, thousands of lives may be affected by your self-view. For their sakes, as well as your own, you must believe what God has to say about you. In the previous chapter, we looked at a list from the Bible that defines who God is. Now let's look at what God has to say about you:

- You are a new creation *(2 Corinthians 5:17)*
- You have a new spirit and a new heart *(Ezekiel 11:19)*

- You have a new nature that is daily being renewed *(Colossians 3:10; 2 Corinthians 4:16)*
- You have been given a new name *(Revelation 2:17; 3:12)*
- You are no longer a slave to sin *(Romans 8:9)*
- You are bought with a price, and belong to God *(1 Corinthians 6:19,20; Psalm 24:1)*
- You are the apple of God's eye *(Zechariah 2:8)*
- You have angels who watch over you and care for you *(Hebrews 1:14; Psalm 34:7)*
- You are to be a blessing to many others *(Genesis 12:2; Galatians 3:14)*
- You are to live an abundant life *(John 10:10)*
- You have an abundance of God's grace and have all of your needs met in God *(2 Corinthians 9:8; Philippians 4:19)*
- You are able to approach God boldly, without fear *(Hebrews 4:16)*
- You are saved by grace and not by your own works *(Ephesians 2:8)*
- You are a child of God *(John 1:12)*
- You are connected to every other believer, and belong to each other *(1 Corinthians 12:13)*
- You are more than a conqueror through Jesus Christ your Lord *(Romans 8:37)*
- You have overcome the world *(1 John 5:5)*
- You bring the Lord pleasure *(Psalm 149:4)*
- You are being made into the image of Christ, looking more and more like Him with each day *(Romans 8:29)*
- You do not lose heart when facing trying times *(2 Corinthians 4:16)*
- You are free from fear *(Romans 8:15)*
- You are comforted by God in discouraging circumstances *(2 Corinthians 7:6)*
- You are able to comfort others and encourage them *(1 Thessalonians 5:11)*

- You are able to be content in all circumstances *(Philippians 4:11)*
- You are growing in your ability to love others *(1 Thessalonians 3:12)*
- You have all things work together for your good *(Romans 8:28)*
- You can do all things through Christ who strengthens you *(Philippians 4:13)*
- You enjoy God's protection and covering *(Psalm 91:4)*
- You have the Lord fight for you *(Exodus 14:14)*
- You have power over God's enemies *(Luke 10:19)*
- You are fully armed for battle *(Ephesians 6:11)*
- You have been given spiritual weapons that are mighty *(2 Corinthians 10:14)*
- You are taught by the Holy Spirit Himself *(Luke 12:12)*
- You are the temple of the Holy Spirit *(1 Corinthians 6:19)*
- You have been given spiritual eyes and ears *(2 Kings 6:17; Proverbs 20:12)*
- You will do greater things than even Jesus did, by His Spirit's power and by His direction *(John 4:12)*
- You are an eternal being, no longer trapped by your mortality *(Romans 8:11)*
- You will sit together in heavenly places with Christ Jesus *(Ephesians 2:6)*

I could go on and on, (some of you thought I already had), because God has a lot to say about you. If you're like me, though, when you look at that list it's easy to say, "That's not me! I'll never live up to all of those things!" But you see, all of these things are yours by faith, by the decree of God, and we receive them not by doing great things, but by believing in the One who describes us this way.

Again, it comes down to a choice. Will you choose to believe your view of yourself, or God's? You must decide who is better-qualified to speak authoritatively on your identity. Will it be God, who formed you and created you, or will it be yourself, who often sees nothing but your own weaknesses and disappointments? Once you accept His view, then you must begin the process of learning how to live according to your new nature. We'll tackle that topic in the next chapter.

CHAPTER 9
DISCUSSION QUESTIONS

What price did God pay for you?

_____

_____

_____

What does that say about your value to Him?

_____

_____

_____

Which of the statements about you listed in this chapter do you agree with the most?

_____

_____

_____

Which do you struggle to agree with the most?

_____

_____

_____

How are you honoring God in the way you take care of yourself?

_____

_____

_____

What changes can you make about how you see yourself based on How much God values you?

_____

_____

_____

LEARNING HOW TO LIVE AS A NEW PERSON

CHAPTER 10

Most of us have lived a long time with an inaccurate self-view, and as a result, have developed a lot of bad habits in the way we live and interact with others. These have to be unlearned and replaced with an entirely different way of being. God stands ready to teach us, and once we accept His authority to determine who we are and who we are to become, He will begin to re-shape us in His image. This is not an automatic process, but requires our willingness and effort to learn a new way of living. Look at how the apostle Paul states it in his letter to the Ephesians:

> *Ephesians 4:17-19 (NLT)*
> *[17]With the Lord's authority let me say this: Live no longer as the ungodly do, for they are hopelessly confused. [18]Their closed minds are full of darkness; they are far away from the life of God because they have shut their minds and*

hardened their hearts against him. ¹⁹They don't
care anymore about right and wrong, and they
have given themselves over to immoral ways.
Their lives are filled with all kinds of impurity
and greed.

When we are the authority in our life, determining our identity, we become hopelessly confused. We end up shutting our minds to the promises of God and the things He is trying to say to us about our future. In this state, we are unable to hear or understand the impact He wants us to have on others, and we end up wasting our lives. Paul goes on to say, however, that we are no longer stuck with that limited viewpoint:

> *Ephesians 4:20-24 (NLT)*
> *²⁰But that isn't what you were taught when you*
> *learned about Christ. ²¹Since you have heard*
> *all about him and have learned the truth that is*
> *in Jesus,²²throw off your old evil nature and your*
> *former way of life, which is rotten through and*
> *through, full of lust and deception. ²³Instead, there*
> *must be a spiritual renewal of your thoughts and*
> *attitudes. ²⁴You must display a new nature because*
> *you are a new person, created in God's likeness—*
> *righteous, holy, and true.*

When we become Christians, Christ begins to teach us a new way of seeing ourselves and everyone around us. He begins by teaching us a new way to think, and then continues by teaching us how to act on those new thoughts. He reminds us that we need to throw off our old way of living, and learn new habits based on our new nature.

One of the best examples of this is seen in the life of a man named Gideon. Gideon, like King Saul, had an improper view of who he was. Though he lived one hundred and fifty years before Saul, he suffered from the same disease of inferiority. However, he ended up much differently, because he was willing to let God teach him how to live:

> Judges 6:11-12 (NLT)
> [11] Then the angel of the LORD came and sat beneath the oak tree at Ophrah, which belonged to Joash of the clan of Abiezer. Gideon son of Joash had been threshing wheat at the bottom of a winepress to hide the grain from the Midianites. [12] The angel of the LORD appeared to him and said, **"Mighty hero, the LORD is with you!" (emphasis mine)**

Notice how God stated His view of Gideon, even though he looked like anything but a hero at the time of this conversation! He was hiding from the enemy, not making plans to lead a rebellion, or a counter attack, but trying to scratch out a living, staying out of the fray. But remember, God's view of us is not based on what we have done in the past, but rather on what we will become for Him as we follow His plan for our lives. Gideon was unconvinced, however, and brushed aside that seemingly inaccurate description of himself. Instead, he complained to God, whining about how God had not been faithful to His people, and inferring that He could not be trusted to keep His word to them:

> Judges 6:13 (NLT)
> "Sir," Gideon replied, "if the LORD is with us, why has all this happened to us? And where are all the miracles our ancestors told us about? Didn't they say, 'The LORD brought us up out of Egypt'? But now the LORD has abandoned us and handed us over to the Midianites."

If God was wrong about His ability to protect them, then how could He be qualified to define Gideon's abilities? But notice

God's response; He simply continued in His teaching process, telling Gideon what the best use of his life would be:

> *Judges 6:14-15 (NLT)*
> *[14]Then the LORD turned to him and said, "Go with the strength you have and rescue Israel from the Midianites. I am sending you!" [15]"But Lord," Gideon replied, "how can I rescue Israel? My clan is the weakest in the whole tribe of Manasseh, and **I am the least in my entire family!"***
> ***(emphasis mine)***

Sound familiar? His response was almost word for word the same as King Saul's. Neither of them felt qualified to do what God was asking them to do, but Gideon, in the end, was willing to let God change his mind about himself:

> *Judges 6:16-17 (NLT)*
> *[16]The LORD said to him, "I will be with you. And you will destroy the Midianites as if you were fighting against one man." [17]Gideon replied, "If you are truly going to help me, show me a sign to prove that it is really the LORD speaking to me.*

Gideon was still unsure, but he asked God to help him believe by showing him a sign, a confirmation that the Lord was able to do this great thing through him. God was more than willing, knowing that Gideon was open to being re-trained in his thinking about God's ability. Take a look at what God did for Gideon:

> *Judges 6:18-21 (NLT)*
> *[18]Don't go away until I come back and bring my offering to you." The LORD answered, "I will stay here until you return." [19]Gideon hurried home. He cooked a young goat, and with half a bushel of flour he baked some bread without yeast.*

*Then, carrying the meat in a basket and the broth
in a pot, he brought them out and presented them
to the angel, who was under the oak tree. ²⁰The
angel of God said to him, "Place the meat and
the unleavened bread on this rock, and pour the
broth over it." And Gideon did as he was told.
²¹Then the angel of the LORD touched the meat and
bread with the staff in his hand, and fire flamed up
from the rock and consumed all he had brought.
And the angel of the LORD disappeared.*

Gideon had certainly never seen anything like that, and he
couldn't deny that God was able to do the impossible. His
faith was growing, and God knew Gideon was ready for a
training assignment. Eventually, God would ask him to take
on the entire Midianite army, but first He gave this young
warrior a more modest assignment. It wasn't without
significant risk, however, and would require great courage and
trust in the Lord:

Judges 6:25-27 (NLT)
*²⁵That night the LORD said to Gideon, "Take the
second best bull from your father's herd, the one
that is seven years old. Pull down your father's
altar to Baal, and cut down the Asherah pole
standing beside it. ²⁶Then build an altar to the
LORD your God here on this hill, laying the
stones carefully. Sacrifice the bull as a burnt
offering on the altar, using as fuel the wood of
the Asherah pole you cut down." ²⁷So Gideon
took ten of his servants and did as the LORD had
commanded. But he did it at night because he
was afraid of the other members of his father's
household and the people of the town. He knew
what would happen if they found out who had
done it.*

God wanted to show Gideon that the secret to his success was not his own might or cunning, but rather that God was first in all he did. He was to lead his family, tearing down false idols and establishing that they would serve God alone. Gideon obeyed, but you can see that fear was still affecting him, since he did it at night to hide from those who would challenge this act. He had not yet arrived, but he was growing in his ability to trust God's instructions and His ways. He was fully engaged in the training process, learning how to act according to his new nature. His actions created real opposition. In fact, the leaders of his city were ready to kill him for what he had done. However, Gideon's own father stood up for him:

> *Judges 6:28-31 (NLT)*
> *[28]Early the next morning, as the people of the town began to stir, someone discovered that the altar of Baal had been knocked down and that the Asherah pole beside it was gone. In their place a new altar had been built, and it had the remains of a sacrifice on it. [29]The people said to each other, "Who did this?" And after asking around and making a careful search, they learned that it was Gideon, the son of Joash. [30]"Bring out your son," they shouted to Joash. "He must die for destroying the altar of Baal and for cutting down the Asherah pole." [31]But Joash shouted to the mob, "Why are you defending Baal? Will you argue his case? Whoever pleads his case will be put to death by morning! If Baal truly is a god, let him defend himself and destroy the one who knocked down his altar!"*

This must have encouraged and strengthened Gideon further. Remember when we looked at Saul's life, we saw that one of the essential equipping ingredients he was given was team members, people willing to follow Saul's lead. Could it be that

Gideon was being shown the same principle? In any case, he was now ready for the next step in his training. The threat to his people had doubled, as the Midianites formed an alliance with another nation in order to attack Israel. But God gave Gideon the most essential part of his equipping, the gift of the Holy Spirit. As we saw in Saul's life, the Spirit of God is what enables us to become who we are destined to be, and that was no more evident than in Gideon's life. Look at the change in his behavior once that wonderful gift is given to him:

> *Judges 6:33-35 (NLT)*
> *[33] Soon afterward the armies of Midian, Amalek, and the people of the east formed an alliance against Israel and crossed the Jordan, camping in the valley of Jezreel. [34] Then the Spirit of the LORD took possession of Gideon. He blew a ram's horn as a call to arms, and the men of the clan of Abiezer came to him. [35] He also sent messengers throughout Manasseh, Asher, Zebulun, and Naphtali, summoning their warriors, and all of them responded.*

No longer hiding in the winepress, concerned only for his own skin, he now boldly called for the rest of the nation to join with him to fight the enemy. He did this in the full light of day, confident that God was with Him and would accomplish His purposes through him. He was really learning how to walk in his new nature! However, as he realized what he had done – that he had "gone public" with God's plan for his life – he began to get nervous. "Have I really heard God? The stakes are really high, Lord. Lots of people's lives hang in the balance. I can't afford to be wrong here, so would you confirm your word to me that you are going to do what you said you would do?" These are the same questions you and I would ask, and no doubt we would need the same assurances from the Lord. God is more than willing to provide what we need. He is committed to our growth, and to His will for our lives. He knows what we need in order to trust Him, and He will build our faith.

I first experienced this principle about a hundred years ago, when I was 19 and just beginning to understand what it was like to have a personal relationship with the Lord. I had drifted off to sleep and had begun to dream an old dream, actually a recurring nightmare I had a lot as a young child. I had not experienced this dream for many years, but it was frightening and real nonetheless. I was at a party, a gathering of adults, and was so young that I only came up to people's waists. They were talking and laughing, but I couldn't understand what they were saying. I was looking for someone, probably my parents, but I felt completely out of my element. As I moved through the room, the conversations and laughter became louder and louder, and the room began to spin and the people became distorted. This continued for what seemed a long time, with the tempo and the noise growing faster and louder, and the figures growing more and more grotesque. In the past, I would eventually wake up soaked in sweat, frightened out of my mind. I experienced real terror this time as well, but just as the dream became unbearable, suddenly the people froze in place and all of the sound ceased. Superimposed over the now still picture was a cartoon bubble, like the kind you see in the funny pages to denote what the characters are saying. It was large enough to obscure most of my field of vision, and in bold letters proclaimed, **"I HAVE CALLED YOU!"** I knew somehow that this was God's voice directed to me, and then a much smaller bubble appeared, with the arrow pointing to me, with my response in very tiny letters, "To what?" His response was merely repeated, louder and more insistent this time, and then I woke up. In my heart I knew that God was calling me to be a pastor, which terrified me! I determined then and there to never tell anyone what I had experienced. For one thing, I was sure they would think I had gone off the deep end, starting to hear voices and such. For another, I was sure God was making a HUGE mistake! I had no idea what it meant to be a pastor, and I had never envisioned or desired such a life. Besides, as a college sophomore, I had my whole career mapped out, and my plans did not have any room for detours dictated to me by some weird dream that was probably the product of bad pizza. But the thing is, the certainty in my heart that I had heard God would not go away. It was all I could think about, and I was doing everything I could NOT to think about it!

Finally, about three months later, I was volunteering down at our little church, helping the pastor do some repairs on the building, when he asked me how things were going in my life. Out of nowhere, and without warning, I blurted out, "Well, I had this weird dream, and I think God is trying to say something to me through it." I was horrified that I had revealed this to anyone, let alone my pastor! He asked me to tell him what I had seen and what I thought it meant, and I again surprised myself by saying, "I think God is asking me to be a pastor!" My pastor just smiled and said, "I think so too; in fact, I've known that is what He wants for you for months." He just didn't say anything to me, wisely believing I needed to hear this first from the Lord. That way, I would not second guess myself later and somehow believe he had talked me into it.

Anyway, my pastor said to me, "Well, we'll have to start your training, and we might as well start right away. Why don't you preach for us this next Wednesday night?" I agreed, but I have to tell you, I was absolutely horrified! You see, I was a fairly shy individual, and didn't like speaking in front of people. Oral reports in school were an ordeal, and I couldn't even imagine having to stand up in front of our church for thirty minutes and somehow have anything worthwhile to say. I sweated bullets, believe me, over the next several days. I had no idea how to write a sermon, and I was sure I was going to make a complete fool of myself. If you had been watching me during those days, you would have thought I was a condemned prisoner with only a few days to live! Nothing was coming together for me; I threw out more pages of notes than my trash can could hold. Then, on the day before I was to speak, I was sitting on the lawn at college and promptly fell asleep, something I had never done before. When I woke up forty minutes or so later, I had my whole sermon in my head! Amazed, I wrote it down furiously. My confidence was still pretty low, but at least I had something I could attempt to deliver without completely embarrassing myself and everyone who would have to endure my first sermon.

When I arrived at the church on Wednesday night, I was a wreck, and it didn't help that the pastor informed me that he expected me to lead the entire service, including the singing portion. Now, it is not false humility that I tell you that singing is simply not one of my gifts, and it certainly wasn't that night. I was so off-key, it was like watching one of those really bad contestants on *American Idol*. I mean, that song service was painful! The people were trying to be gracious, but you know how it is when you have to suffer through someone else making a complete fool of themselves – just recalling the memory is making me queasy! Needless to say, by the time I finished with the songs and the announcements, I wanted to crawl under a rock and die. But then an amazing thing happened. I stepped up to the pulpit to bring the sermon, and it was like a mantle rested on my shoulders. I can only describe it this way; I have never felt more "me" than at that moment. I was infused with confidence, and as I began to speak I felt as if I was born to do this. It was like an out-of-body experience; I was listening to myself and thinking, "Wow, that's really good – where did that come from?"

I knew somehow that what I was saying was not coming from me, but directly from the Lord, and I was the most amazed person in the room. As soon as I finished, however, it was as if that mantle had lifted, and I became afraid that the people would "find me out," that they would in time discover that I was not that smart, not that eloquent, that somehow I had just gotten lucky, and if they were to hear me again, they would get a performance more like my singing debut. People were telling me that they felt God had spoken directly through me, but rather than be encouraged, I became more and more depressed.

From then on, the cycle seemed to repeat itself. I would botch the song service, experience the strange sense of confidence when I brought the sermon, and the same sense of fear that I would run dry by the next time I was asked to speak. This went on for months, and I was growing more and more miserable. I just didn't understand what was happening, that God had indeed given me a calling and a gift, and my success did not depend on me and my abilities, but on Him. I still felt that God had made a mistake, and that He should have called someone more qualified. The more people tried to encourage me, the more pressure I felt to perform. I didn't know what to do about this, when God spoke to me again, this time in a service at our church. Our pastor finished his sermon, and then he invited anyone who wanted more from God to come to the altar and pray. I was the first one there, I was so desperate! As I began to pray and ask God to take this "calling" away, I saw a picture in my mind, as clear as day. There was a beautifully wrapped gift held in two huge hands, being offered to me. Once again, I somehow knew those were God's hands and He was giving this gift to me. As I reached up to take the gift from Him, I was horrified to see myself reach right past the hands and slap God in the face! I broke down immediately, for I finally understood what had been happening to me. God was offering me a gift, to preach and lead His people, and in my lack of confidence and by focusing on my inability and inexperience, I was rejecting that gift. I realized in that moment how hateful and foolish that was, and I told God that if He would forgive me, I would give Him the rest of my life. I would hold nothing back, but would serve Him with all of my heart. Never again would I reject His will for my life, whether I understood it or not. I told Him I still thought He was making a mistake in asking me to do this, but that He had every right to me and my life. From that day to this, He has been faithful to our agreement. I covet those times when I hear His voice clearly, and trust His ability to use someone as limited as I am. There are still lots of times when I question why He would want to use me, and times when it seems hard to hear His voice. But through it all, I am learning that He will keep fine-tuning my ability to know what He wants me to do.

See how He continues this learning process for Gideon:

> *Judges 6:36-40 (NLT)*
> [36] *Then Gideon said to God, "If you are truly going to use me to rescue Israel as you promised,* [37] *prove it to me in this way. I will put some wool on the threshing floor tonight. If the fleece is wet with dew in the morning but the ground is dry, then I will know that you are going to help me rescue Israel as you promised."* [38] *And it happened just that way. When Gideon got up the next morning, he squeezed the fleece and wrung out a whole bowlful of water.* [39] *Then Gideon said to God, "Please don't be angry with me, but let me make one more request. This time let the fleece remain dry while the ground around it is wet with dew."* [40] *So that night God did as Gideon asked. The fleece was dry in the morning, but the ground was covered with dew.*

Gideon was almost ready to fulfill his destiny. By now, he had seen God do the impossible, and had seen how God protected him from an angry mob. He had seen his confidence grow, and had been emboldened to call others to join him in his quest. Only one more step remained. Sometimes, when we begin to get a few victories under our belt, we make the mistake of trusting in ourselves, or in the resources we have at our disposal. We may forget that God gives us everything we need for victory, and we may begin to count on the things He provides rather than on Him. This has disastrous consequences, not just for our own destiny, but for those we are leading. God is about to do Gideon a tremendous favor. He is going to whittle away at his army, until there were so few that any victory would certainly be accredited to God, rather than Gideon. This was not done because God wanted all the credit, but because he knew Gideon, like us, was not built to withstand the pressure of his accomplishments. If the people believed Gideon was solely responsible for their victory, they would begin to expect bigger and bigger things from him. If, however, they understood that God was clearly the reason for his success, they would put their trust in God, not in Gideon. That would be good for them, and for Gideon. He would not collapse under the burden of other people's expectations, as King Saul did. Instead, because God caused him to be completely dependent on Him, that weight would fall on God's shoulders, where it belongs. He is more than strong enough to handle it:

> *Judges 7:2-7 (NLT)*
> *[2]The LORD said to Gideon, "You have too many warriors with you. If I let all of you fight the Midianites, the Israelites will boast to me that they saved themselves by their own strength. [3]Therefore, tell the people, 'Whoever is timid or afraid may leave and go home.' "Twenty-two thousand of them went home, leaving only ten thousand who were willing to fight. [4]But the LORD told Gideon, "There are still too many! Bring them down to the spring, and I will sort out who will go with you and who will not." [5]When Gideon took his warriors down to the water, the LORD told him, "Divide the men into two groups. In one group put all those who cup water in their hands and lap it up with their tongues like dogs. In the other group put all those who kneel down and drink with their mouths in*

*the stream." [6]Only three hundred of the men drank
from their hands. All the others got down on their
knees and drank with their mouths in the stream.
[7]The LORD told Gideon, "With these three hundred
men I will rescue you and give you victory over the
Midianites. Send all the others home."*

To his credit, Gideon obeyed. He was convinced by this time
that God was able to do the impossible, and so he followed
what the Lord told him to do. He did not concern himself with
what the people would think of his leadership, as Saul did. He
was only concerned with what God thought about him, and
apparently God had decided to deliver His people through
Gideon and his small band of men. After God saw Gideon's
obedience, He provided an additional faith builder for him. He
told Gideon to go to the enemy's camp that night and
eavesdrop on their conversation. He would be greatly
encouraged by what he heard, for the Lord had put a fear of
Gideon in the enemy's hearts:

> *Judges 7:9-15 (NLT)*
> *[9]During the night, the LORD said, "Get up! Go
> down into the Midianite camp, for I have given
> you victory over them! [10]But if you are afraid
> to attack, go down to the camp with your servant
> Purah. [11]Listen to what the Midianites are saying,
> and you will be greatly encouraged. Then you will
> be eager to attack." So Gideon took Purah and went
> down to the outposts of the enemy camp. [12]The
> armies of Midian, Amalek, and the people of the
> east had settled in the valley like a swarm of locusts.
> Their camels were like grains of sand on the
> seashore—too many to count! [13]Gideon crept up
> just as a man was telling his friend about a dream.
> The man said, "I had this dream, and in my dream a
> loaf of barley bread came tumbling down into the
> Midianite camp. It hit a tent, turned it over, and*

knocked it flat!" ¹⁴His friend said, "Your dream
can mean only one thing—God has given Gideon
son of Joash, the Israelite, victory over all the
armies united with Midian!" ¹⁵When Gideon
heard the dream and its interpretation, he
thanked God. Then he returned to the Israelite
camp and shouted, "Get up! For the LORD has
given you victory over the Midianites!"

Now, what are the odds that Gideon would be passing by those two guys, at that exact moment, when they were discussing this dream? Out of all the tents in the Midianite camp, he just "happened" to go by that one? And these great warriors were frightened to death by a loaf of bread? Can you imagine Gideon's thoughts at that moment? "Thanks, God, that you're going ahead of us and ensuring the enemy is convinced of their doom, but a loaf of bread? Couldn't you have depicted us as a mighty lion, or giant warriors?" It is as if God was going out of His way to show Gideon, that even though you think you are nothing, I am with you and you and I together are completely unbeatable!

Gideon did prevail over the enemy, using God's plan of attack. The plan asked Gideon and his men to arm themselves only with pitchers and torches, so it would be clear who provided the victory. Gideon obeyed, and presided over one of the biggest upsets in all of history! The people were delivered from a great oppression, and went on to make Gideon their leader. He fulfilled his destiny on the earth, because he was willing to let God change his mind about the way he saw himself.

God is so thorough in helping us become who He has destined us to be. Knowing us inside and out, He provides all we need in order for us to believe Him. He equips us to grow into our new nature, helping us to develop new habits of carrying ourselves before Him and people. This is true not just for those called to lead whole nations, as Gideon and Saul were. God is determined to use all of us, and gives us influence in the lives of the people around us. To use that influence for their good, we must be willing to receive all that He has for us, and believe that He wants to use us to be a blessing to others. We will all struggle with feelings of inadequacy, even the most gifted among us. But it would be a great waste of our lives if we focused on our lack of ability rather than on God's limitless supply!

Which long-held views of yourself need another look?

_____

_____

_____

What attitude adjustments do you most need to make when it comes to how you see yourself?

_____

_____

_____

What new stories do you need to tell yourself about you that will line up more consistently with God's view of you?

_____

_____

_____

What changes do you need to make in order to have God first in your life?

_____

_____

_____

What processes does God currently have you in to help you change how you see yourself?

_____

_____

_____

CHAPTER 11

SO, WHO DO YOU THINK *YOU* ARE?

CHAPTER 11

It's too bad that Saul didn't go to school on Gideon. If he had studied this leader of Israel's life, he would have seen that his value was in God and not in his own abilities. He, like Gideon, would have been able to overcome his sense of inferiority, and would have led his people so much better. He would have realized his true value, and the people would have been the benefactors.

But it wasn't just Gideon's story that was available to him. So many other leaders had gone before him, and all of them had to deal with their own inadequacies. Moses felt inadequate to lead God's people due to a stuttering problem, and a track record of failure as a deliverer of his people. Nevertheless, God used him to become Israel's first great emancipator. He went on to become a giant in the people's eyes, a leader who spoke to God face to face and lived to tell about it! Joshua had the unenviable task of following in Moses' footsteps. Who wouldn't feel intimidated by trying to measure up to that great leader? Yet God assured him that He would be with him just as He was with Moses. Joshua chose to believe God, and became a great leader in his own right. He was responsible for leading the people into the Promised Land, giving them a home of their own for the very first time. Caleb, Joshua's friend and colleague, was one who figured out that the source of his strength was God Himself. He had stood by Joshua's side for years, helping him lead the people into their new home. At the ripe old age of 85, Caleb made this declaration:

> *Joshua 14:10-11 (NLT)*
> [10]*"Now, as you can see, the LORD has kept me alive and well as he promised for all these forty-five years since Moses made this promise—even while Israel wandered in the wilderness. Today I am eighty-five years old. [11]I am as strong now as I was when Moses sent me on that journey, and I can still travel and fight as well as I could then."*

Now Caleb almost certainly was not as strong physically at 85 years of age as he was when he was 40. But notice his last statement in verse 12:

> *Joshua 14:12 (NLT)*
> *"So I'm asking you to give me the hill country that the LORD promised me. You will remember that as scouts we found the Anakites living there in great, walled cities. **But if the LORD is with me,** I will drive them out of the land, **just as the LORD said." (emphasis mine)***

He knew that the source of his strength had always been the Lord being with him, and the fact that the Lord had said he would use him to drive out the enemy. He had always known this. Forty-five years earlier, Moses had sent him and Joshua, along with ten other men, to scout the land that God had promised to give them. They found a land filled with all the good things God had said it would have, but also an abundance of skilled and seasoned fighting men. Joshua and Caleb insisted they could overcome the opposition, not because they were stronger, but because the Lord had said they would. He had promised to be with them, and that was all the proof they needed. Unfortunately, the other ten men chose not to believe God's promises, and convinced the people not to follow God's instructions. As a result, they were not allowed to enter the land until all of the adults had died off, except Joshua and Caleb. Look at God's assessment of Caleb at that time:

> *Numbers 14:24 (NIV)*
> *But because my servant Caleb has a different spirit and follows me wholeheartedly, I will bring him into the land he went to, and his descendants will inherit it.*

Caleb had settled in his heart whose opinion would guide his life. Since God had promised to be with them, and had instructed them to take over this new land, that was what he would do. His own shortcomings were a non-factor, and it was not necessary that he be stronger than the opposition he faced. He no doubt knew that the enemy was physically stronger and more experienced in warfare. But the source of his strength was God Himself, and that was more than enough. That is why he could say with integrity at the advanced age of 85 that he was just as strong then as in his younger days. God was still with Him, and His promises were still to be trusted. Therefore, these enemies, though formidable, would fall to the might and power of God. Caleb and his entire family did go on to conquer their land, and all the people benefited greatly.

Saul knew all of these stories, and yet he chose to determine his value based on his own view of things. But what about you and me? Will we make the same mistake? Or will we choose to let God's opinion of us be the one we accept as truth? You see, we have the same choice set before us today. In fact, we have even more examples than Saul did of lives that have gone before us. God encourages us to make the right choice, to focus on Jesus rather than ourselves so we can run the race of life successfully:

> *Hebrews 12:1-2 (NLT)*
> *[1]Therefore, since we are surrounded by such a huge crowd of witnesses to the life of faith, let us strip off every weight that slows us down, especially the sin that so easily hinders our progress. And let us run with endurance the race that God has set before us. [2]We do this by keeping our eyes on Jesus, on whom our faith depends from start to finish.*

We all have flaws. We all have baggage. We all have reasons to believe we cannot accomplish the dreams God has placed within our hearts. We know instinctively that apart from God we will never achieve the great things we long to achieve. But the good news is that He has promised to never leave us or forsake us. He has promised to accept us just as we are, and to equip us with everything we will need to accomplish what He asks us to do. He will give us a team of like-minded people to help us, and He will give us His Spirit to help us focus on Jesus instead of the obstacles.

Remember, your decision will impact many other people. Will you invite Him to change the way you think about you? Will you let Him train you to walk in your new nature and understanding? Will you accept His authority to declare your worth and value? And will you let His Word determine the course of your life? The stakes are high, so choose well, my friend!

CHAPTER 11
DISCUSSION QUESTIONS

Whose story of transformation most inspires you?

_____

_____

_____

Which mentors have you chosen to include in your life to help you see yourself more accurately?

_____

_____

_____

In what ways have you changed your mind about yourself as a result of this book?

_____

_____

_____

Who can you share these insights with?

_____

_____

_____

A FINAL
WORD

It may be that you have never invited God into your life. You may even attend church, read your Bible, and volunteer to help others around you. You have tried to be a good person, but you have never really surrendered your life to Him. You realize that you have allowed your opinion to rule over your life instead of God's, and you would like that to change. All that is needed is for you to ask God to come into your heart. You are the only one who can surrender your will to Him – and He invites you to do so today!

Simply pray a prayer like this one:

Lord Jesus, I invite you to come into my life. I know that I can never accomplish the great things you have for me without You. Show me how to live my life Your way, and I will follow what you ask me to do. Forgive me for trying to go it alone, without you. I now know how pointless that is. Thank you for loving me!

If you prayed that prayer, congratulations! I invite you to tell someone what you did, and to begin to learn His ways for living. Embrace His opinion of you, and let Him begin to share with you His plan for your life. May God bless you as you become a blessing to many!

To contact the author about speaking at your conference or church, please email info@donroberts.org.

Made in the USA
San Bernardino, CA
29 August 2018